Air Fryer Cookbook:

5 Ingredients or Less.
Easy and Delicious Air Fryer Recipes for Your Family

Sandy N. Jones

Disclaimer

The recipes and information in this book are provided for educational purposes only. Please always consult a licensed professional before making changes to your lifestyle or diet.

The author and/or publisher shall have neither liability nor responsibility to anyone with respect to any loss or damage caused, or alleged to be caused, directly or indirectly by the information contained in this book. All trademarks and brands within this book are for clarifying purposes only and are owned by the owners themselves, not affiliated with this document.

Air Fryer Cookbook:

5 Ingredients or Less. Easy and Delicious Air Fryer Recipes for Your Family

Table of Contents

Air Fryer Cookbook:

5 Ingredients or Less. Easy and Delicious Air Fryer Recipes for Your Family

Air Fryer Cookbook:

5 Ingredients or Less. Easy and Delicious Air Fryer Recipes for Your Family

Introduction

With the air fryer, you can still enjoy all of your favorite foods without all of the fat and calories. The air fryer takes the fat out of frying, but it still provides you with the great taste that you love. Now you can eat healthily and not feel as if you are depriving yourself.

This book is going to provide you with tons of recipes specifically created for your air fryer. You will not only find all of your favorite foods in this book, but you will also find many new recipes that I am sure you will love.

On top of this, you are going to find that the air fryer is going to help you reduce the calories in all of your meals while allowing you to enjoy great food with tons of flavor.

Chapter 1: How to Properly and Safely Use the Air Fryer

Everyone has been raving about the new air fryer lately and while you may have just purchased yours, or you may still be considering purchasing one, it is important that you know exactly how to use it.

The great news is that no matter what level your culinary skills are at, you can use the air fryer and you can use it to cook almost anything.

Why are people so excited about the air fryer?

People love fried foods, but we all know how bad frying foods in fat or oil can be. Fried foods taste amazing, but they are packed full of calories. This is where the air fryer is able to help. The air fryer is able to provide you with the foods that you love such as fried chicken, onion rings, and even French fries while reducing the number of calories in the foods.

While most healthy options for these types of foods, lack flavor or leave a bad taste in one's mouth, the air fryer, provides you with the same great taste, same great crunch but with fewer calories. It allows you to eat the foods that you love but in a healthy way.

Not only are you able to cook your favorite fried foods with the air fryer but you can also broil, bake, grill and roast in the

Air Fryer Cookbook:

5 Ingredients or Less. Easy and Delicious Air Fryer Recipes for Your Family

air fryer.

The air fryer allows you to cook without the use of fats or oils and it is able to cook several items at the same time. On top of all of this, the air fryer is easy to take apart and clean.

Ways to Use the Air Fryer

One of the things that people love the most about grilling in the air fryer is that they do not have to stand over the grill and continually flip what they are grilling in order to ensure that it is cooking evenly.

Because the air in the air fryer flows up and around the food, it is able to cook all of the sides at the same time, and all you have to do is in the middle of the cooking time, just shake the pan. When you purchase most air fryers, they will come with a grill pan with a handle which makes it very easy for you to insert it into your air fryer. On top of this, the surface of the grill is going to soak up any fat or other drippings that come from the meat which means that you are only going to be left with healthy grilled meat that you didn't have to monitor while cooking.

Most air fryers are going to also come with baking pans which will allow you to bake muffins, bread, cakes and even brownies right in your air fryer.

The air fryer will also allow you to roast your food in about

20 percent less time than it would take you using other cooking methods.

Of course, the air fryer can be used to fry your favorite foods using not oil but... You guessed it, air. The air fryer is going to ensure that your foods still taste the same as they would if they were fried in fat or oil, they are going to be just as crispy. **However, they are going to have up to 80 percent less fat!**

While many people do take advantage of the oil-less frying, you can still use oil in the foods that you are cooking. The only difference is that if you are going to use oil, it will be on the food itself and not in a vat. Most oils are fine to use with the air fryer.

What Types of Foods Can Be Cooked In the Air Fryer?

Many people who have purchased or who are considering purchasing an air fryer find themselves asking what they can cook in it. The good news is that the air fryer can cook almost any food that you would normally cook on the top of the stove or in a deep fryer for 40 minutes or less.

You can cook any food that can be fried, roasted, baked or grilled. Foods that are breadcrumb coated or lightly coated with flour are best for air frying while those that require a batter should not be cooked in the air fryer.

Air Fryer Cookbook:

5 Ingredients or Less. Easy and Delicious Air Fryer Recipes for Your Family

What Types of Foods Cannot be Cooked in the Air Fryer?

As I already stated, you should avoid cooking anything in the air fryer that has been coated with any type of batter. You should also avoid cooking any vegetable that you would normally steam such as carrots or broccoli.

While there are a few foods that you cannot cook in the air fryer, the foods that you can cook far outnumber them.

The most common food that is cooked in the air fryer is potatoes. You can make French fries from fresh or from frozen; you can make grilled potatoes, tots and the list goes on.

How To Cook Multiple Foods at Once.

On top of all of this, you can use the divider to cook two foods at the same time. The only thing that you need to make sure of is that you do not cook two foods that should be cooked at different temperatures.

You do not want to risk one food not getting heated to the proper temperature, and if you were to cook two foods at that same time that did not require the same cooking temperature, they simply would not cook evenly, and both would not cook to completion.

How Does the Air Fryer Work?

The air fryer works by using hot air circulation. After you place your foods into the basket, you will set the temperature on the air fryer. The hot air is going to then flow around the food that you have placed into the basket, and while cooking the inside of the food, ensuring that it is soft and moist, it is also going to cook the outside of the food crispy and crunchy.

There are even some air fryers that use air filters to prevent the smell of your cooking food from filling your home. While there are some foods that are lovely to smell when you are cooking them, there are others such as fish that we just don't want our homes, our clothes or ourselves smelling like.

Air Fryer Parts

Of course, we have the main appliance part of the air fryer; then we have the pan which has been created to fit perfectly into the air fryer. Next, there is a basket that you can place into the pan. The basket has a handle which will allow you to shake what you are cooking during the process.

The rest of the parts will depend on the brand and the model that you purchase, but you may also receive a divider, a baking tin, and a double grill layer.

The divider is going to be used to allow you to cook two foods

Air Fryer Cookbook:

5 Ingredients or Less. Easy and Delicious Air Fryer Recipes for Your Family

at that same time. However, as stated earlier you have to ensure that these two foods can be cooked together, you need to make sure that they should be cooked at the same temperature.

The baking tin is going to allow you to bake your favorite treats, such as brownies, cookies, and even muffins.

If you want to fry a food, you will need to place it in the basket. The basket will then fit into the pan, and the two together are going to fit perfectly in the air fryer. When you are ready to remove the basket from the pan, you will want to make sure that the pan is sitting on a completely flat surface.

After you have used the air fryer, you will want to allow at least 30 minutes for everything to cool before moving them to the dishwasher. All of the parts are non-stick, and you can wash them in the dishwasher.

Why Shake the Basket?

It is important that if you are cooking more than one item, such as two pieces of chicken, that you shake the basket in the middle of the cooking cycle. This is going to ensure that the two pieces do not get stuck together and it is going to ensure that they cook evenly.

If you do not shake the basket, you will find that the areas where the foods were touching were not reached by the air and did not cook evenly.

Air Fryer Troubleshooting

Air fryer will not turn on- If your air fryer is on, you will see a green light, the red light means that the air fryer is heating up. If your air fryer is not turning on, there are a few things that you can do. First, you will want to ensure that the air fryer is plugged in. Next, check the cord to ensure that it is in good condition and then make sure that the power source is working. Finally, set the time to three minutes to allow the air fryer to preheat then check it to see if it is turned on.

The outside of the air fryer is becoming hot while you use it- If you find that the outside of the air fryer is becoming hot when it is in use, you should not worry. While you are using the fryer, you should only be touching the buttons or the handles. The fryer should be kept in an area where only Adult can reach it because the outside can become very hot and can be dangerous to children.

White smoke is coming from the air fryer while in use- When you are cooking foods that contain a high percentage of fat, you might notice that white smoke will rise from the air fryer. This is because the oil is being caught in the pan and once the oil is heated up, it will cause white smoke.

You can avoid this white smoke by not cooking foods in the air fryer that have a high-fat content. If you notice that the smoke is coming out of the air fryer while you are cooking,

Air Fryer Cookbook:

5 Ingredients or Less. Easy and Delicious Air Fryer Recipes for Your Family

turn the fryer off. Take the pan out of the fryer and then take the basket out of the pan. Using heavy-duty paper towels, soak the oil up from the pan. Once the pan is clean, you can put the basket back in the pan and continue cooking.

How To Insert the Pan in the Fryer

It is important for you to remember that when you insert the pan into the air fryer, you are going to hear a click once it is in place. If you find that you are having a hard time getting the pan into the air fryer, check to ensure that the basket is positioned properly inside of the pan. It is also important to make sure that you have not overfilled the basket, that the food is not coming out of the basket.

Will Everything I Cook Be Crispy?

Not every food that you cook in the air fryer is going to come out crispy as if it had been deep fried. For example, if you cook vegetables in the air fryer, they are not going to be crispy. However, when you cook foods such as meat or potatoes, they will become crispy. It is also suggested that you add a layer of breadcrumbs to the foods that you want to be extra crunchy.

The air fryer is a great alternative to a deep fryer; it is great for grilling foods when you don't really want to grill but want that great flavor, it is an awesome alternative to the stove top as well as the oven.

An air fryer is a great appliance for those that want or need to get healthy but don't want to give up the flavor or the crispiness of their favorite foods.

Air Fryer Safety

It is very important for you to understand the air fryer and for you to know how to be safe while using it. It is also important that you ensure that you are using the air fryer properly because if you do not, you increase your risk of injury.

The great thing about the air fryer is that because it does not require oil to cook the foods, it is quite safe. However, there are a few things that you should know. The first thing, we discussed a moment ago, and it is that the outside of the air fryer gets very hot. You should make sure that the appliance is out of reach of children and that no one touches it while it is on.

Make sure that you never rinse or clean by submerging in water the actual appliance, the housing or the electrical components. Getting any of this wet could cause a person to suffer from shocks which could end up being lethal.

Do not fill the pan with oil. The air fryer has been designed to work without oil and adding oil can cause a fire hazard.

Air Fryer Cookbook:

5 Ingredients or Less. Easy and Delicious Air Fryer Recipes for Your Family

Avoid touching the inside of the air fryer and the hot area while it is in use. Not only is this going to protect you from burns as we have already discussed, but it is also going to ensure that you do not put yourself at risk for being shocked in the event that the appliance malfunctions.

Do not cover the inlets and outlets while you are using the air fryer. If you cover these, there is not going to be any way for the air to enter or escape the air fryer and this can put you in great danger.

Keep the power cord away from hot surfaces, including the air fryer itself. If the cords are exposed to excessive heat, they can become damaged and present a hazard.

Make sure that your hands are dry while you are operating the appliance and make sure that you do not place anything on top of the appliance. You also need to make sure that the air fryer is placed on a level, flat surface that is stable. This will ensure that the air fryer does not get knocked down while it is being used possibly burning a child or pet.

When you are removing the pan from the air fryer, you need to make sure that you are aware of the steam and it is best if you use a pot holder to protect your hand from the steam. Make sure that you clean and maintain the air fryer to prevent any damage. As stated earlier, cleaning is quite simple, and all of the parts are dishwasher safe.

When you use the air fryer properly, you do not have to worry about getting injured or causing damage to the air fryer. Most accidents occur when a person tries to use it in a way that it is not designed to be used, for example adding oil to the pan.

Air Fryer Cookbook:

5 Ingredients or Less. Easy and Delicious Air Fryer Recipes for Your Family

Chapter 2: Cooking Conversion Chart

MEASUREMENT

CUP	ONCES	MILLILITERS	TABLESPOONS
8 cup	64 oz	1895 ml	128
6 cup	48 oz	1420 ml	96
5 cup	40 oz	1180 ml	80
4 cup	32 oz	960 ml	64
2 cup	16 oz	480 ml	32
1 cup	8 oz	240 ml	16
3/4 cup	6 oz	177 ml	12
2/3 cup	5 oz	158 ml	11
1/2 cup	4 oz	118 ml	8
3/8 cup	3 oz	90 ml	6
1/3 cup	2.5 oz	79 ml	5.5
1/4 cup	2 oz	59 ml	4
1/8 cup	1 oz	30 ml	3
1/16 cup	1/2 oz	15 ml	1

WEIGHT

IMPERIAL	METRIC
1/2 oz	15 g
1 oz	29 g
2 oz	57 g
3 oz	85 g
4 oz	113 g
5 oz	141 g
6 oz	170 g
8 oz	227 g
10 oz	283 g
12 oz	340 g
13 oz	369 g
14 oz	397 g
15 oz	425 g
1 lb	453 g

Air Fryer Cookbook:

5 Ingredients or Less. Easy and Delicious Air Fryer Recipes for Your Family

TEMPERATURE

FAHRENHEIT	CELSIUS
100 °F	37 °C
150 °F	65 °C
200 °F	93 °C
250 °F	121 °C
300 °F	150 °C
325 °F	160 °C
350 °F	180 °C
375 °F	190 °C
400 °F	200 °C
425 °F	220 °C
450 °F	230 °C
500 °F	260 °C
525 °F	274 °C
550 °F	288 °C

Sandy N. Jones

Air Fryer Cookbook:

5 Ingredients or Less. Easy and Delicious Air Fryer Recipes for Your Family

Chapter 3- Side Dishes

Not only can you cook your favorite meats and main courses with the air fryer but you can also cook all of your favorite fried side dishes without all of the oil which means that the side dishes that you have grown to love are going to have fewer calories ad still taste as great as you have always remembered.

Brussels Sprouts

Serves 2. Prep Time: 10 Mins, Cook Time: 10 Mins

Temperature: 400 °F

You will need:

2 cups of brussels sprouts that have been cut in half lengthwise

1 tablespoon of olive oil

1 tablespoon of balsamic vinegar

1/4 of a teaspoon of sea salt

Directions:

Toss the Brussels sprouts in a bowl with the rest of the ingredients and toss until the sprouts are coated well and evenly. Cook for 10 minutes in the air fryer at 400 degrees and shake after 5 minutes and then again after 8 minutes. They should look browned and crispy but not burnt.

Air Fryer Cookbook:

5 Ingredients or Less. Easy and Delicious Air Fryer Recipes for Your Family

Curly Fries

Serves 2. Prep Time: 10 Mins, Cook Time: 20 Mins Temperature: 390 °F

You will need:

2 medium Potatoes, cleaned

1 tablespoon of olive oil

1 teaspoon of salt plus a bit more for seasoning

Salt and pepper for taste

Directions:

1. Begin by cutting the ends off of the potatoes using a very sharp knife. Using a spiralizer and a thick blade, spiralize each potato.

2. Place the spiralized potatoes in a mixing bowl and drizzle 1 tablespoon of olive oil on them as well as 1 teaspoon of salt. Toss to ensure they are coated well.

3. Place 1/2 of the potatoes in the air fryer basket and preheat the air fryer to 390 degrees. After the air fryer preheats, cook for 15 minutes. If they are not done

after 15 minutes, shake the basket and continue to cook for an additional 5 minutes.

4. After the fries have cooked, remove them from the basket and season them with salt while they are still hot. Place the potatoes on a baking sheet and place them in an oven at 200 degrees in order to keep them warm while you cook the second batch.

5. You can dip it with your favorite sauce.

Air Fryer Cookbook:

5 Ingredients or Less. Easy and Delicious Air Fryer Recipes for Your Family

Pigs in a Blanket

Serves 2. Prep Time: 10 Mins, Cook Time: 7 Mins

Temperature: 400 °F

You will need:

6 hot dogs

1 tube of 9 refrigerated biscuit dough

BBQ aioli

1:1 of BBQ sauce and Mayo combined

Directions:

1. Begin by cutting each of the hot dogs into thirds. Remove the biscuits from the tube and cut each of them in half.

2. Flatten each of the halves of the biscuits, slightly.

3. Wrap each third of hotdog in 1/2 of a biscuit and pinch the seams together to ensure they are closed. Place the pigs in a blanket seam side down in the basket and preheat the air fryer to 400 degrees.

4. After the air fryer has preheated, cook the pigs in a blanket for 7 minutes, shaking after 4 minutes.

Bacon Cashews

Serves 2. Prep Time: 10 Mins, Cook Time: 8-10 Mins

Temperature: 350 °F

You will need:

3 cups of raw whole cashews

2 teaspoons of salt

2 tablespoons of blackstrap molasses

3 tablespoons of liquid smoke

Directions:

1. Mix all of the ingredients together in a large bowl ensuring that the cashews are coated very well and evenly.

2. You will then pour the coated cashews into the air fryer basket and cook them for 8-10 minutes at 350 degrees. Make sure that you shake them every 2 minutes to ensure that they cook evenly. During the last two minutes of cooking, you need to shake them once per minute to ensure that they do not burn.

3. Let the cashews cool after they are done cooking and store them in an airtight container or serve.

Air Fryer Cookbook:

5 Ingredients or Less. Easy and Delicious Air Fryer Recipes for Your Family

Buffalo Cauliflower

Serves 2. Prep Time: 10 Mins, Cook Time: 15 Mins Temperature: 350 °F

You will need:

4 cups of cauliflower florets

1 cup of breadcrumbs mixed with a teaspoon of sea salt

1/4 of a cup of melted butter

1/4 of a cup of your favorite buffalo sauce

For dipping, you can use, mayo, cashew ranch or any other salad dressing

Directions:

1. Begin by melting the butter in the microwave and then whisking it in a bowl with the buffalo sauce. Hold each of the cauliflower florets by the stem and then dip them into the buffalo sauce mixture, coating as much of the floret as you can in the sauce. Hold the floret over the bowl until it stops dripping.

2. Roll the floret in the breadcrumbs coating as much as you would like. After you have done this to all of the

florets, place them in the basket and into the air fryer. Cook for 15 minutes at 350 degrees and shake every five minutes.

3. Serve these with the dipping sauce of your choice.

Hasselback Potatoes

Serves 2. Prep Time: 10 Mins, Cook Time: 35 Mins

Temperature: 370 °F

You will need:

2 large Russet potatoes that have been washed

2 teaspoons of salt

2 tablespoons of Extra virgin olive oil

Directions:

1. You will begin by placing one of the potatoes between two chopsticks and then slice it into thin slices. Be sure to leave 1/2 of an inch at the bottom unsliced. (don't slice all the way through) The chopsticks on each side are to ensure that you do not slice all the way through.

2. Do the same thing to the second potato. Next, drizzle the potatoes with the olive oil and sprinkle with salt. Cook for 15 minutes at 370 degrees. Remove the potatoes from the air fryer and drizzle them with more olive oil and sprinkle with more salt. Place back in the air fryer and continue to cook for another 15 minutes. Repeat this one more time and then cook for 5 minutes. Serve with sour cream.

Potato Chips

Serves 2. Prep Time: 20 Mins, Cook Time: 15 - 20 Mins

Temperature: 300 °F

You will need:

2 potatoes, large

Olive oil in a spray bottle

Sea salt and black pepper

Directions:

1. Begin by washing the potatoes. Do not peel them. Slice the potatoes into slices that are about 1/8 of an inch thick. After they are sliced, you will rinse them in cold water until the water begins running clear. Next, soak the potato slices in a large bowl of cold water for no less than 10 minutes.

2. After the potatoes have soaked, you will drain them and place them on a kitchen towel in a single layer.

3. Next, you are going to preheat the air fryer to 300 degrees. While the air fryer is preheating, you will want to spray the potatoes with the oil ensuring that both sides are coated evenly. If you do not have a

Air Fryer Cookbook:

5 Ingredients or Less. Easy and Delicious Air Fryer Recipes for Your Family

spray bottle, coat your hands in oil and rub the potato slices between them.

4. You are going to cook these in two separate batches for 15 -20 minutes and shake the basket every 5 minutes. When the chips have cooked, you will season them with sea salt and ground pepper.

5. Dip it with your favorite sauce

Crispy Roasted Broccoli

Serves 2. Prep Time: 10 Mins, Cook Time: 12 Mins

Temperature: 400 °F

You will need:

500 grams of fresh broccoli

1 teaspoon of chickpea flour

For the marinade, you will need:

2 tablespoons of plain yogurt

1/4 of a teaspoon of turmeric

1/2 of a teaspoon of salt

1/2 of a teaspoon of red chili powder

Directions:

1. Begin by cutting the broccoli into small florets. Place the broccoli in a bowl of water with 2 teaspoons of salt to remove all of the impurities or parasites.

Air Fryer Cookbook:

5 Ingredients or Less. Easy and Delicious Air Fryer Recipes for Your Family

2. Remove the broccoli from the water and drain it well. Dry by using a kitchen towel to ensure all of the moisture has been absorbed.

3. Place all of the marinade ingredients in a bowl and mix well.

4. Place the florets into the marinade, ensuring all of them have been coated evenly.

5. Cover the bowl and allow to soak for 15 minutes in the refrigerator.

6. After the broccoli has marinated, you will want to preheat your air fryer to 400 degrees. Place the broccoli into the air fryer basket and place the basket in the air fryer.

7. Set the timer for 10 minutes, shaking the basket after 5 minutes. Check after 10 minutes so see if the broccoli is golden brown and crispy. If it is not, cook for an additional 2 to 3 minutes.

8. Serve hot.

Apple Chips

Serves 4. Prep Time: 10 Mins, Cook Time: 10 Mins

Temperature: 360 °F

You will need:

6 red apples

1 teaspoon of olive oil

1 pinch of ground cinnamon

Directions:

1. Begin by chopping your apples into chunks that are bite sized.

2. Place the apples in the air fryer basket and drizzle one teaspoon of olive oil on them.

3. Cook at 360 degrees for 10 minutes. Place them in a bowl with the cinnamon and toss.

Air Fryer Cookbook:

5 Ingredients or Less. Easy and Delicious Air Fryer Recipes for Your Family

Fried Pickle Chips

Serves 4. Prep Time: 15 Mins, Cook Time: 20 Mins Temperature: 350 °F

You will need:

One 32 ounce jar of whole dill pickles, large

2 eggs

2/3 of a cup of panko breadcrumbs

1/3 of a cup of freshly grated parmesan cheese

1/4 of a teaspoon of dried dill weed

Directions:

1. Begin by slicing the pickles lengthwise into slices that are about 1/4 of an inch thick. Place the pickles between paper towels and pat them dry.

2. Place the eggs in a shallow bowl and beat them until they are smooth.

3. Place the breadcrumbs, dill weed, and parmesan cheese in a zip lock back and shake well to ensure that they are completely mixed.

4. Place 4-5 slices of pickle in the eggs ensuring that they are completely coated. Allow the excess egg to drip off.

5. Place the pickles in the bag with the breadcrumbs and shake well.

6. Place 1/2 of the pickles that have been coated into the air fryer and cook for 8 to 10 minutes at 350 degrees. Remove the pickles and cook the second half. Serve with ranch dressing.

Air Fryer Cookbook:

5 Ingredients or Less. Easy and Delicious Air Fryer Recipes for Your Family

Avocado Fries

Serves 4. Prep Time: 10 Mins, Cook Time: 10 Mins

Temperature: 390 °F

You will need:

1/2 of a cup of panko breadcrumbs

1/2 of a teaspoon of salt

1 avocado that has been peeled, pitted and cut into slices

The liquid from One 15 ounce can of either white or garbanzo beans

Directions:

1. Place the panko breadcrumbs and the salt in a bowl. Mix well. Place the liquid from the beans into another bowl.

2. Dip the avocado slices in the liquid then carefully roll them in the breadcrumbs ensuring that they are coated evenly.

3. Place the avocado slices in the air fryer basket in a single layer. Make sure that none of them overlap.

4. Cook for 10 minutes at 390 degrees, shaking after 5 minutes.

5. Serve hot with dipping sauce.

Baked Garlic and Parsley Potatoes

Serves 4. Prep Time: 10 Mins, Cook Time: 40 Mins

Temperature: 390 °F

You will need:

3 baking potatoes

1 to 2 tablespoons of olive oil

1 tablespoon of salt

1 tablespoon of parsley

1 tablespoon of garlic

Directions:

1. Begin by washing your potatoes and then poking them with a fork to create air holes.

2. Drizzle a bit of olive oil over the potatoes then rub it over the skin. Sprinkle the seasonings on the potato and rub it over the skin to ensure it is coated evenly.

3. Place the potatoes in the air fryer basket and cook for 40 minutes at 390 degrees. Serve immediately with your favorite toppings.

Air Fryer Cookbook:

5 Ingredients or Less. Easy and Delicious Air Fryer Recipes for Your Family

Chapter 4- Appetizers

Using the air fryer, you can make all of the foods that you want for any meal including appetizers in no time at all, without using any oil and reducing the number of calories in the foods that you cook.

Spiced Nuts

Serves 2. Prep Time: 10 Mins, Cook Time: 25 Mins

Temperature: 300 °F

You will need:

1 egg white that has been beaten lightly

1/2 of a cup of sugar

1 teaspoon of salt

1/4 of a teaspoon of allspice

Pinch ground pepper

1 cup of raw pecan halves

1 cup of raw cashew halves

1 cup of raw almonds

Directions:

1. Begin by mixing the spices, the sugar and the egg white in a medium-sized bowl. Next, you will want to go ahead and preheat your air fryer to 300 degrees.

2. Place all of the nuts in the bowl with the egg and spices and toss until they are evenly coated. Spray

Air Fryer Cookbook:

5 Ingredients or Less. Easy and Delicious Air Fryer Recipes for Your Family

your basket with nonstick cooking spray and place your nuts in the basket. Place everything in the air fryer and cook for 25 minutes, shaking every five minutes. After 25 minutes, check to ensure that the nuts are crunchy but be careful because they will be very hot. Serve warm or allow to cool before serving. These can be stored in a container that is airtight for about 2 weeks.

Buffalo Wings

Serves 4. Prep Time: 10 Mins, Cook Time: 26 Mins

Temperature: 400 °F

You will need:

2 LBS. of chicken wings

3 tablespoons melted butter

¼ of a cup of Frank's Hot Sauce

Salt

Directions:

1. Begin by cutting off the tips of the wings and discarding them. Next, you will want to separate the drumettes and wingettes and place them in a bowl.

2. Mix the butter and the Franks Hot Sauce in a separate bowl and ensure that they are blended well. Pour this over the wings and allow them to marinate for 2 hours or overnight.

3. After the wings have marinated, you will preheat your air fryer to 400 degrees for about 3 minutes. Cook them one batch at a time, wingettes then drumettes for 12 minutes each shaking every 5 minutes. After the second batch is done cooking, you will then place the

Air Fryer Cookbook:

5 Ingredients or Less. Easy and Delicious Air Fryer Recipes for Your Family

first batch in the basket with the second and continue to cook them both for another 2 minutes.

Sweet and Salty Snack Mix

Serves 4. Prep Time: 10 Mins, Cook Time: 25 Mins

Temperature: 370 °F

You will need:

1/2 of a cup of honey

3 tablespoons of melted butter

1 teaspoon of salt

2 Cups of mini pretzels

2 cups of sesame sticks

1 cup of pumpkin seeds

1 cup of raw cashews

Directions:

1. Begin by mixing the honey, salt, and butter in a small bowl. Stir well to ensure that it is completely combined.

2. Next, you will want to place the pumpkin seeds, sesame sticks, cashews and pretzels in a large bowl and mix well. After these have been mixed, pour the

Air Fryer Cookbook:

5 Ingredients or Less. Easy and Delicious Air Fryer Recipes for Your Family

honey mixture over the top and toss well to ensure that everything is coated evenly.

3. Preheat your air fryer to 370 degrees and place 1/2 of the mixture into the basket air frying for 12 minutes. Shake the basket every two minutes while this is cooking. Then cook the second batch.

4. After the mix is done cooking, you will place it on a cookie sheet in a single layer and allow it to cool. This can be stored in a container that is airtight for one week.

Reuben Egg Rolls

Serves 2. Prep Time: 10 Mins, Cook Time: 14 Mins

Temperature: 400 °F

You will need:

Egg Roll wrappers

Sliced corned beef

1 can of sauerkraut

Sliced Swiss cheese

Oil spray of your choice

Make as many rolls as you want

Directions:

1. Begin by cutting your sliced corned into narrow strips. Cut the Swiss cheese into narrow strips.

2. Drain all of the liquid off of the sauerkraut and use a paper towel to absorb any leftover liquid.

3. Place one egg roll wrapper in front of you, with the corner pointed towards you. Moisten the sides of the egg roll wrapper with a bit of water to ensure that it seals.

Air Fryer Cookbook:

5 Ingredients or Less. Easy and Delicious Air Fryer Recipes for Your Family

4. Place the corned beef and Swiss cheese in the wrapper. If your corned beef is thin, you will want to use a few slices per layer. Create two layers of the cheese and corned beef making a stack.

5. Add in a bit of sauerkraut and then fold the end of the wrapper that is pointed towards to over the beef, cheese, and sauerkraut.

6. Fold both sides in and roll the rest of the wrapper up.

7. Spray the egg roll on both sides using your oil and place it in the air fryer basket. Preheat your air fryer to 400 degrees.

8. When you are placing the egg rolls in the basket, you might find you want to cook in batches, depending on how many you are cooking. You want to give them a bit of room so that they are not pressed against each other.

9. Cook the rolls for 7 minutes and then flip them. Cook them for an additional 7 minutes.

10. Serve with thousand island dressing.

Buttery Dinner rolls

Serves 8. Prep Time: 25 Mins, Cook Time: 10 - 20 Mins

Temperature: 360 °F

You will need:

1 cup of milk at room temperature

114 grams of softened butter

63 grams of sugar

2 eggs

1.5 teaspoons of salt

508 grams of all-purpose flour

2 1/4 teaspoons of instant yeast

You will also need some extra butter to use as a glaze.

Air Fryer Cookbook:

5 Ingredients or Less. Easy and Delicious Air Fryer Recipes for Your Family

Directions:

1. Place all of your ingredients in your mixer in the order that they are listed and set the mixer to the dough setting.

2. After the mixer has run, you will lightly flour your surface and punch the air out of the dough.

3. Divide your dough into 18 evenly sized portions and create balls with them. Place the baking sheet in the air fryer basket and using non-stick cooking spray, spray the sides of the basket as well as the baking sheet. Place 9 balls in the basket and allow to sit for an additional 30 minutes or until they have doubled in size.

4. Preheat your air fryer to 360 degrees and bake the rolls for 10 minutes or until they are golden brown.

5. **Half the recipe if you only want to make 1 batch.**

6. After they have baked, brush them with the melted butter.

Apple Dumplings

Serves 2. Prep Time: 15 Mins, Cook Time: 25 Mins

Temperature: 360 °F

You will need:

2 small apples

2 tablespoons of raisins

1 tablespoon of brown sugar

2 tablespoons of melted butter

2 puff pastry sheets

Directions:

1. Begin by preheating your air fryer to 360 degrees. Peel and core your apples. Place the raisins and the brown sugar in a bowl and mix well.

2. Place each of the apples on one of the pastry sheets and then using the brown sugar and raisin mixture, fill up the core.

3. Fold the pastry over the apple ensuring that it is completely covered.

Air Fryer Cookbook:

5 Ingredients or Less. Easy and Delicious Air Fryer Recipes for Your Family

4. Place a small piece of foil in the bottom of the air fryer basket to ensure that if any of the filling does come out, it will not end up in your air fryer. Place the dumplings in the basket and brush with butter

5. Cook for 25 minutes. Serve hot.

Chapter 5 – Breakfast

Not only can you cook your dinner and your appetizers in your air fryer but you can also cook all of your favorite breakfasts with no oil which means that you are going to be reducing the amount of calories you consume even when you are eating your breakfast.

Air Fryer Cookbook:

5 Ingredients or Less. Easy and Delicious Air Fryer Recipes for Your Family

Tofu Scramble

Serves 2. Prep Time: 10 Mins, Cook Time: 30 Mins

Temperature: 370 - 400 °F

You will need:

1 block of medium to firm tofu that has been cut into pieces that are about 1" cubes.

2 tablespoons of soy sauce

2 tablespoon of olive oil

1/2 of a teaspoon of garlic powder

1/2 of a cup of onions, chopped

4 cups of broccoli florets

2.5 cups of chopped potato

Directions:

1. You will begin by placing the tofu cubes, 1 tablespoon of oil, soy sauce, garlic powder and chopped onion in a bowl. Mix well and then set to the side and allow to marinate.

2. You will place the chopped potatoes in a separate bowl and toss them with the other tablespoon of oil until they are coated evenly. Place the potatoes in the air

fryer basket and cook for 15 minutes, at 400 degrees and shake after 7 minutes.

3. After the potatoes have cooked for 15 minutes, you will shake them again and then add in the tofu. Reserve the leftover marinade. Cook this for 15 minutes at 370 degrees. While you are cooking the tofu and the potatoes, place the broccoli florets in the marinade, adding a bit of extra soy sauce if needed.

4. After the potatoes and tofu have cooked for 10 minutes, toss in the broccoli and finish cooking for the last 5 minutes. Serve hot.

Air Fryer Cookbook:

5 Ingredients or Less. Easy and Delicious Air Fryer Recipes for Your Family

Breakfast Sausage and Cheese Wrap

Serves 2. Prep Time: 15 Mins, Cook Time: 8 Mins

Temperature: 380 °F

You will need:

8 sausage

1 can of crescent dough, 8 count

2 slices of American cheese that has been cut into four pieces each

8 skewers, must be wooden

Syrup or ketchup to dip the wraps in

Directions:

1. Place the crescent rolls on a flat surface place 1/4 of a piece of cheese on each crescent roll, and one sausage. Roll the sausage up in the crescent roll, starting with the widest part of the triangle. Pinch all of the dough around the sausage.

2. Preheat the air fryer to 380 degrees and cook four wraps in the basket and cook for 4 minutes. Remove the wraps and add the skewer. Cook the next four.

3. Serve hot with your favorite dip

Breakfast Frittata

Serves 2. Prep Time: 15 Mins, Cook Time: 10 Mins

Temperature: 360 °F

You will need:

3 eggs

1/2 of an Italian sausage

4 cherry tomatoes, halved

Fresh chopped parsley

1 tablespoon of olive oil

Parmesan Cheese

Salt and pepper

Directions:

1. Begin by preheating your air fryer to 360 degrees. After the air fryer has preheated, you will toss the cherry tomatoes, and sausage into the baking accessory and cook for 5 minutes. While this is cooking, you will whisk all of the other ingredients together in a bowl.

Air Fryer Cookbook:

5 Ingredients or Less. Easy and Delicious Air Fryer Recipes for Your Family

2. After the sausage and tomatoes have cooked for 5 minutes, you will pour the egg mixture over them and continue to cook for another 5 minutes.

3. Serve hot.

Scrambled Eggs

Serves 2. Prep Time: 10 Mins, Cook Time: 4 Mins

Temperature: 400 °F

You will need:

1/2 of a cup of heavy cream

1 tablespoon of sunflower oil

3 eggs

Salt and pepper

Directions:

In a bowl, you will mix the eggs, cream, and the salt. Then scramble them. Coat your baking dish with the 1 tablespoon of sunflower oil and then pour the eggs in. Bake at 400 degrees for 4 minutes. Salt and pepper to taste and serve hot.

Air Fryer Cookbook:

5 Ingredients or Less. Easy and Delicious Air Fryer Recipes for Your Family

Skillet Potatoes

Serves 2. Prep Time: 10 Mins, Cook Time: 20 Mins

Temperature: 400 °F

You will need:

1 tablespoon of onion powder

1 tablespoon of paprika

3 potatoes

Salt and pepper

Directions:

1. First, you will want to peel the potatoes and cut them into 1" cubes. Rinse the cubes and pat them dry. Place them in a bowl and sprinkle the onion powder, 1 tablespoon of sunflower oil, and the paprika over the top. Toss well to ensure that the potatoes are coated evenly.

2. Place the potatoes in the basket and cook for 20 minutes at 400 degrees, shaking every 5 minutes. After they have cooked, serve hot.

Air Baked Eggs

Serves 2. Prep Time: 10 Mins, Cook Time: 20 Mins

Temperature: 350 °F

You will need:

7 ounces of ham sliced

1 pound of baby spinach

4 eggs

1 tablespoon of olive oil

Unsalted butter

Salt and pepper to taste

Directions:

1. Begin by preheating your air fryer to 350 degrees. Then butter your baking dish. On the stove top, you will place the olive oil and the and heat the baby spinach on medium heat until it wilts. After the spinach wilts, you will drain all of the excess liquid off.

2. Place the spinach in your baking pan and top with the ham. Crack one egg in each corner of the pan. Sprinkle with salt and pepper. Cook for 20 minutes and serve hot.

Air Fryer Cookbook:

5 Ingredients or Less. Easy and Delicious Air Fryer Recipes for Your Family

Baked Egg In a Bread Bowl

Serves 4. Prep Time: 10 Mins, Cook Time: 25 Mins

Temperature: 350 °F

You will need:

4 dinner rolls

4 eggs

4 tablespoons of parsley, chives, and tarragon mixed

4 tablespoons of heavy cream

Salt and pepper

Grated Parmesan Cheese

Directions:

1. You will begin by cutting the top off of the dinner rolls and taking some of the bread out create a hole which will hold the egg. Place the rolls on a baking sheet.

2. Crack one egg into each roll and sprinkle each egg with 1 tablespoon of the mixed herbs. Use salt and pepper if desired and finish with a bit of grated parmesan cheese.

3. Preheat your air fryer to 350 degrees and cook the bread and eggs for 20 minutes. After the eggs have cooked for 20 minutes, you will take the bowls out of the air fryer and place the tops on the rolls. Cook for another five minutes and then take them out of the air fryer. Let the rolls sit for 5 minutes before serving.

Air Fryer Cookbook:

5 Ingredients or Less. Easy and Delicious Air Fryer Recipes for Your Family

Breakfast Soufflé

Serves 2. Prep Time: 10 Mins, Cook Time: 8 Mins

Temperature: 390 °F

You will need:

4 eggs

4 tablespoons of light cream

Red chili pepper, chopped finely

Fresh Parsley chopped

Directions:

1. Place the eggs in a bowl and mix in the red chili pepper, cream, and the fresh parsley. Fill your soufflé dishes half way with the mixture. Preheat the air fryer to 390 degrees and cook the soufflés for 8 minutes.

2. Serve hot.

Breakfast Sandwich

Serves 1. Prep Time: 10 Mins, Cook Time: 6 Mins

Temperature: 390 °F

You will need:

1 egg

1 Canadian bacon

1 English muffin

Salt and pepper to taste

Directions:

Begin by preheating the air fryer to 390 degrees. Crack the egg into your ovenproof soufflé cup, then place the muffin, egg and the bacon into the air fryer. Cook for 6 minutes. After everything has cooked for 6 minutes, assemble the sandwich. You may also want to add a slice of cheese.

Air Fryer Cookbook:

5 Ingredients or Less. Easy and Delicious Air Fryer Recipes for Your Family

Full English

Serves 4. Prep Time: 10 Mins, Cook Time: 18 Mins

Temperature: 390 °F

You will need:

8 chestnut mushrooms

8 cherry tomatoes, halved

4 slices of smoked bacon

4 chipolatas

2 cups of baby spinach

4 eggs

Directions:

Begin by preheating your air fryer to 390 degrees. Place the mushrooms and halved tomatoes in a round baking tin and spray with oil. Season with your favorite seasonings. Place this in the air fryer and cook for about 10 minutes.

While the vegetables are cooking, you will want to wilt your spinach in the microwave and mix it with the eggs. After the vegetables have cooked, pour the egg mixture over them and reduce the temperature to 300 degrees. Cook the eggs for 8 minutes. Serve hot.

Cheese and Tomato Toast

Serves 1. Prep Time: 5 Mins, Cook Time: 5 Mins

Temperature: 360 °F

You will need:

2 slices of bread

1 slice of your favorite cheese

4 tomato slices

Butter

Pepper

Directions:

1. Begin by buttering 1 side of each slice of bread and then make your sandwich with the buttered side of the bread on the outside.

2. Preheat your air fryer to 360 degrees. Place the sandwich in the air fryer and cook for 4 minutes.

3. Remove the sandwich, add more butter and continue to cook for an additional minute.

4. Serve hot.

Air Fryer Cookbook:

5 Ingredients or Less. Easy and Delicious Air Fryer Recipes for Your Family

Egg in a Basket

Serves 1. Prep Time: 10 Mins, Cook Time: 8 Mins

Temperature: 360 °F

You will need:

2 slices of bread

2 tablespoon of butter

2 eggs

Salt and pepper

Directions

1. Using a glass, press the open part into each slice of bread to cut a circle out. Preheat your air fryer to 360 degrees for 5 minutes after placing the pan into the air fryer.

2. After the air fryer has heated, place 1 tablespoon of butter into the pan and allow to melt.

3. Place the bread into the pan after the butter has melted. Crack one egg into each of slices of bread ensuring that the egg is inside of the hole in the bread.

4. Sprinkle with salt and pepper.

5. Cook for 5 minutes.

6. Remove the bread and egg from the pan. Place 1 tablespoon of butter in the pan and allow to melt. Place the bread back in the air fryer, opposite side down. Sprinkle with salt and pepper and cook for an additional three minutes.

7. Serve hot.

Air Fryer Cookbook:

5 Ingredients or Less. Easy and Delicious Air Fryer Recipes for Your Family

Chapter 6 – Meat Recipes

There are many types of meat that you can cook in your air fryer, but in this chapter, I want to focus on beef, pork and lamb. We will go over poultry recipes later on in the book.

Roasted Pork Loin and Potatoes

Serves 4. Prep Time: 10 Mins, Cook Time: 35 Mins

Temperature: 390 °F

You will need:

2 pounds pork loin

2 large red potatoes diced

1 teaspoon of salt

1 teaspoon of pepper

1/2 of teaspoon of garlic powder

1/2 of a teaspoon of red pepper flakes

Directions:

1. Begin by putting the salt, pepper, garlic powder and red pepper flakes in a small bowl. Then sprinkle the seasoning mixture over the pork loin and the diced potatoes. Place the potatoes and the pork loin in the basket and then in the air fryer. Set the timer for 35 minutes and the temperature to 390 degrees.

2. Shake the basket every 5 minutes while the pork loin and potatoes are cooking. After the timer goes off, you will take the pork loin out of the basket and let it rest on a plate before you slice it. While you are letting the

Air Fryer Cookbook:

5 Ingredients or Less. Easy and Delicious Air Fryer Recipes for Your Family

loin set, place the potatoes on a plate. Slice the pork loin and then place 5 slices over the potatoes. Serve immediately.

Easy Rib Eye Steak

Serves 4. Prep Time: 10 Mins, Cook Time: 15 Mins

Temperature: 400 °F

You will need:

2 pounds of rib eye steak

1 tablespoon of your favorite steak rub

1 tablespoon of olive oil

Directions:

1. Begin by preheating the air fryer.

2. While the air fryer preheats, you will rub the steak with oil on both sides then rub the steak rub on both sides of the steak.

3. Put the steak in the basket and the basket into the air fryer. Adjust the cooking time to 15 minutes and temperature to 400 degrees. Flipping the steak after 7 minutes.

4. When the steak is done cooking, you will remove the steak and place it on a plate. Let the steak rest for 10 minutes before slicing. Serve after slicing.

Air Fryer Cookbook:

5 Ingredients or Less. Easy and Delicious Air Fryer Recipes for Your Family

Beef Roll Up

Serves 4. Prep Time: 15 Mins, Cook Time: 14 Mins Temperature: 400 °F

You will need:

2 pounds of beef flank steak

3 tablespoons of pesto

6 slices of Provolone cheese

3 ounces of roasted red bell peppers

3/4 of a cup of fresh baby spinach

1 teaspoon of sea salt

1 teaspoon of black pepper

Directions:

1. Begin by butterfly cutting the steak and then spreading the pesto evenly over one entire side of the steak

2. Next, make a layer of cheese, then a layer of roasted red peppers and finally a layer of spinach. Roll the beef up and secure it in place using toothpicks. Season the outside of the roll using salt and pepper.

3. Place the beef roll into the basket and place in the air fryer. Adjust the time to 14 minutes and temperature to 400 degrees, rotate the meat after 7 minutes.

4. After the beef has cooked, you are going to place it on a plate and then let it rest for 10 minutes before you cut it. Serve immediately.

Air Fryer Cookbook:

5 Ingredients or Less. Easy and Delicious Air Fryer Recipes for Your Family

Burgers

Serves 4. Prep Time: 15 Mins, Cook Time: 10 Mins
Temperature: 350 °F

You will need:

1 pound of ground beef, extra-lean

1 tablespoon of Worcestershire sauce

1 teaspoon of Maggi sauce

1/2 of a teaspoon of garlic powder

1/2 of a teaspoon of salt

1/2 of a teaspoon of black pepper

Directions:

1. Begin by mixing the garlic powder, Worcestershire sauce, Maggi sauce, garlic powder, salt and pepper in a small bowl.

2. Place the beef in a large bowl and then add in the spice mixture. Work the spice mixture into the beef ensuring that it is mixed throughout all of the beef evenly.

3. Create four patties with the beef and then press your thumb into the center of each patty to ensure that they do not bunch up in the middle while cooking. Place the burgers in the basket ensuring that they are not touching each other.

4. Preheat your oven to 350 degrees and cook the patties for 10 minutes, shaking after 5 minutes. There is no need for you to flip the burgers while they are cooking. Serve hot on a bun.

Air Fryer Cookbook:

5 Ingredients or Less. Easy and Delicious Air Fryer Recipes for Your Family

Roast Beef

Serves 4. Prep Time: 15 Mins, Cook Time: 30 Mins

Temperature: 300 °F

You will need

2 pounds beef for roasting

1 tablespoon of oil

Cracked pepper or a seasoning of your choice

Directions:

1. Begin by preheating the air fryer to 300 degrees. While the air fryer is preheating, place the roast in a bowl and rub the oil all over the entire roast. After the roast has been covered with oil, you will rub whatever seasoning you want to use all over it as well.

2. After the air fryer has preheated, you will place the roast into the basket and then into the air fryer. Set the time for 30 minutes.

3. After the roast cooks for 30 minutes, take it out of the air fryer and turn it over, then place it back in the air fryer for another 15 minutes.

4. While the roast is cooking, you can make the rest of your meal such as mashed potatoes.

5. If you want the roast to be cooked more than medium rare, you will add 5 minutes at a time and cook it until it is cooked to your preference.

Air Fryer Cookbook:

5 Ingredients or Less. Easy and Delicious Air Fryer Recipes for Your Family

Chinese Roast Pork

Serves 4. Prep Time: 2 Hours, Cook Time: 15 Mins

Temperature: 350 - 400 °F

You will need:

2 pounds pork shoulder

2 tablespoons of sugar

1/3 of a cup of soy sauce

1 tablespoon of honey

1/2 of a tablespoons of salt

Directions:

1. Begin cutting the meat into slices that are 1.5 of an inch wide

2. Create the marinade by mixing the sugar, soy sauce, honey and salt. Then mix the marinade into the meat for 2 minutes before refrigerating the meat in the marinade for at least 2 hours or overnight.

3. After the meat has marinated, you will preheat your air fryer to 350 degrees and place the meat in the

basket. Place the basket in the air fryer for 10 minutes shaking after 5 minutes.

4. After the meat has cooked for 10 minutes, increase the temperature to 400 degrees and cook for 5 more minutes to caramelize it.

Air Fryer Cookbook:

5 Ingredients or Less. Easy and Delicious Air Fryer Recipes for Your Family

Simple Pork Chops

Serves 4. Prep Time: 15 Mins, Cook Time: 15 Mins

Temperature: 350 °F

You will need:

4 pork chops that are about 3/4 of an inch thick

1/2 of a cup of Dijon mustard

1/2 of a cup of Italian seasoned breadcrumbs

1 teaspoon of salt

1 teaspoon of pepper

Directions:

1. Begin my coating the pork chops thickly with the Dijon mustard. Next you will want to mix the breadcrumbs, salt and pepper in a small bowl. Coat the pork chops in the bread crumbs and then place them in the basket.

2. Carefully spray the chops with a bit of the oil spray. Preheat the air fryer to 350 degrees and place the basket in the air fryer. Cook for 10 minutes, shaking after 5. After the pork chops have cooked for 10

minutes, remove the basket, turn the chops over and spritz them one more time with the oil.

3. Place them back into the air fryer and continue to cook for another 5 minutes.

Air Fryer Cookbook:

5 Ingredients or Less. Easy and Delicious Air Fryer Recipes for Your Family

Crispy Roasted Pork Belly

Serves 4. Prep Time: 12 Hours, Cook Time: 45 Mins Temperature: 350 - 370 °F

You will need:

2 pound pork belly

3 teaspoons of salt

2 teaspoons of sugar

1/2 of a teaspoon of five-spice powder

Directions:

1. Begin by scraping away the impurities as well as the hair that are on the pork belly using a sharp knife. Rinse the pork belly to ensure all of the impurities are gone and then set it to the side.

2. Next you will want to mix the salt, sugar and the five spiced powder in a bowl, then set to the side as well.

3. Place a pot of water on the stove top and bring the water to a boil. Blanch the pork in the water until it is about 70 percent of the way done or for about 15 minutes. You want to ensure that the skin is softened.

4. After you have blanched the pork, drain it and pat it dry using paper towels or a kitchen towel. Next you will want to cut a few slits into the pork which will ensure that it absorbs the seasonings.

5. Rub the seasonings on the pork, ensuring that the meat is coated evenly, but you do not want to place any on the rind because the five-spice will cause it to be dark.

6. Make sure you wipe the rind off and then using a steel skewer, you will poke as many holes in the rind as you can.

7. Place the meat in aluminum foil, wrapping it around all of the meat except for the rind. Place this in the fridge and allow the rind to dry overnight. After the meat has set in the fridge overnight, you will take it out and let it rest at room temperature for 30 minutes. Again, poke the rind with the skewer and then wipe the rind to ensure there are no spices on it.

8. Preheat your air fryer to 350 degrees and place the pork belling into the basket with the skin up. Cook this for 20 minutes. After 20 minutes, you will take it out of the air fryer, wipe the rind once more and then place it back in the air fryer, increasing the temperature to 370 and cooking for an additional 25 minutes.

Air Fryer Cookbook:

5 Ingredients or Less. Easy and Delicious Air Fryer Recipes for Your Family

Easy Rack of Lamb with Breadcrumbs

Serves 4. Prep Time: 20 Mins, Cook Time: 30 Mins

Temperature: 250 - 380 °F

You will need:

1 clove of garlic

1 tablespoon of olive oil

1.5 pound rack of lamb

1 tablespoon of pepper

Breadcrumbs as needed

1 egg

Directions:

1. You will begin by chopping up the clove of garlic and mixing it with the oil. Coat the rack of lamb with the garlic and oil mixture then use the pepper to season the rack of lamb.

2. Preheat your air fryer to 250 degrees. While the air fryer is preheating, you will beat the egg.

3. Dip your rack of lamb into the beaten egg and then allow the excess egg to drip off. After dipping the rack of lamb in the egg, you will roll it in the breadcrumb.

4. Place the rack of lamb in your air fryer basket and cook for 25 minutes. After cooking for 25 minutes, you will increase the temperature to 380 degrees and cook for an additional 5 minutes.

5. Serve it with your favorite vegetables.

Air Fryer Cookbook:

5 Ingredients or Less. Easy and Delicious Air Fryer Recipes for Your Family

Lamb Rump Mini Roast

Serves 4. Prep Time: 15 Mins, Cook Time: 35 Mins

Temperature: 350 - 390 °F

You will need:

1.5 pound lamb rump

1 clove of garlic, crushed

Dried rosemary

3 potatoes that have been washed, peeled and then cut in half

2 teaspoons of olive oil

Directions:

1. Begin by rubbing the crushed garlic on the lamb rump. After rubbing it with garlic, you will sprinkle the rosemary all over the lamb rump.

2. Place the divider into the air fryer basket and place the lamb rump on one side. Preheat your air fryer to 350 degrees and place the lamb in the air fryer for 20 minutes.

3. While the lamb is cooking, you will place your potatoes in the microwave and cook them for 4 minutes and then drain off any excess water.

4. Coat the potatoes in a bit of oil.

5. After the lamb has cooked for 20 minutes, you will put the potatoes. Increase the temperature to 390 degrees and cook for 15 minutes, shaking every 5 minutes.

6. After cooking, slice the lamb and serve it with the vegetables.

Air Fryer Cookbook:

5 Ingredients or Less. Easy and Delicious Air Fryer Recipes for Your Family

Honey and Mustard Pork Balls

Serves 2. Prep Time: 10 Mins, Cook Time: 15 Mins

Temperature: 390 °F

You will need:

1/2 of a pound of minced pork

1/4 of an onion, diced

1 teaspoon of mustard

1 teaspoon of honey

A handful of basil, chopped

Salt and pepper

Directions:

1. Place all of the ingredients in a large bowl and mix well. Preheat your air fryer to 390 degrees. While the air fryer is preheating, form the meat mixture into balls. Place the balls in the air fryer basket and cook for 15 minutes. You will only want to cook one layer at a time so if you find you have more balls than this, you will want to cook in batches.

2. Serve hot.

Cheese Burger

Serves 2. Prep Time: 5 Mins, Cook Time: 15 – 25 Mins

Temperature: 360 °F

You will need:

250 grams of ground beef

1 onion

1 teaspoon of your favorite mixed herbs

100 grams of cheddar cheese

Salt and pepper

Directions:

1. Begin by preheating your air fryer to 360 degrees.

2. Next, you are going to finely dice the onion. Place the diced onion, ground beef, and your seasoning into a large bowl and mix well.

3. Roll the beef into 4 balls that are the same size and them flatten them down until they are very thin.

4. Place 2 of the cheese on two of the burgers and then place another burger on each of them. Press the edges

Air Fryer Cookbook:

5 Ingredients or Less. Easy and Delicious Air Fryer Recipes for Your Family

together, creating two burgers filled with cheese. Do the same for the other burger as well.

5. Place the two burgers in the in the air fryer basket and place the basket in the air fryer. Cook for 15 minutes.

6. After they have cooked for 15 minutes, you will want to check to ensure that the juices run clear and that the cheese has melted. You can do this by sticking a knife in the center of one burger.

7. If the burgers are thick and need to cook longer, cook for an additional 10 minutes.

8. Serve on a bun with your favorite toppings.

Chapter 7 – Fish and seafood

Fish is very good for you, and it is a very healthy food for you to eat, however, when you cook it in the air fryer, it is even more healthy! The air fryer can literally cook anything that you want to eat and not only can it reduce the number of calories that you are eating each day but it can also help to make you healthier.

Air Fryer Cookbook:

5 Ingredients or Less. Easy and Delicious Air Fryer Recipes for Your Family

Grilled Fish

Serves 2. Prep Time: 10 Mins, Cook Time: 13 Mins Temperature: 300 - 350 °F

You will need:

2 Small fish

Salt and pepper

Directions:

1. Begin by removing the intestines from each of the fish and wash them well. Pat them dry. Place the salt and the pepper, (as much as you desire) in a small bowl and rub it into the inside of the fish. Let this sit for 30 minutes.

2. After the fish has marinated, place them in the air fryer basket and cook at 300 degrees for 5 minutes. After the first 5 minutes, you will increase the temperature to 350 degrees and cook for another 8 minutes. Serve the fish with your favorite hot sauce.

Fish and chips

Serves 4. Prep Time: 15 Mins, Cook Time: 12 Mins

Temperature: 350 °F

You will need:

2 pounds of red potatoes

1.5 pounds of white fish such as cod

1.4 of a cup of crushed tortilla chips

1 egg

1 tablespoon of vegetable oil

1/2 of a tablespoon of freshly squeezed lemon juice

Directions:

1. Begin by preheating your air fryer to 350 degrees. Cut your fish into 4 pieces. Then rub them with salt and pepper. Squeeze lemon juice over them and then let them set for 5 minutes.

2. Place the crushed tortilla chips on a plate. You can crush them by placing them in a food processor.

3. Place the egg into a dish and beat it. Begin by dipping each piece of fish into the egg and then rolling then in

Air Fryer Cookbook:

5 Ingredients or Less. Easy and Delicious Air Fryer Recipes for Your Family

the crushed tortilla chips. Make sure that each fillet is completely coated in tortilla chips.

4. Wash your potatoes, peel them and then slice them into thin strips. Place the potatoes in clean, cool water and let them soak for about a half of an hour. After they have soaked, place them on paper towels and pat them to ensure that they are dry.

5. Drizzle the vegetable oil over them and then place the separator into the basket. Place the fish on one side of the basket and the potatoes on the other side of the basket.

6. Place the basket in the air fryer and cook for 12 minutes.

Cocktail Prawns

Serves 4. Prep Time: 10 Mins, Cook Time: 8 Mins

Temperature: 350 °F

You will need:

12 King prawns

1 teaspoon chili powder

1 teaspoon chili flakes

1/2 of a teaspoon of black pepper

1/2 of a teaspoon of salt

Directions:

1. Begin by preheating your air fryer to 350 degrees. Mix the chili powder, chili flakes, pepper and salt together in a bowl. Place the prawns into the bowl with the spices and toss them well to ensure that they are evenly coated.

2. Place them into the air fryer basket and then into the air fryer. Cook the prawns for 8 minutes, shaking after 4 minutes.

3. Serve the prawns hot with your favorite dipping sauce.

Air Fryer Cookbook:

5 Ingredients or Less. Easy and Delicious Air Fryer Recipes for Your Family

Salmon Quiche

Serves 4. Prep Time: 15 Mins, Cook Time: 20 Mins

Temperature: 300 °F

You will need:

1.5 pounds of salmon cut into small cubes

1 cup of all-purpose flour

1/2 of a cup of butter that is cold and has been cut into cubes

3 tablespoons of whipping cream

2 eggs and 1 egg yolk

1 green onion, chopped

Salt and pepper

Directions:

1. You will begin by preheating your air fryer to 300 degrees. In a bowl, while the air fryer is preheating you will mix the salt, pepper, and salmon. After mixing the salmon, you will allow it to sit for 10 minutes.

2. While the salmon is resting, you are going to mix the egg yolk and the butter in a bowl. Add in one tablespoon of water and the flour. Knead the dough and create a ball. Flour the counter and then roll the dough out.

3. Place the dough in a quiche pan and trim the edges off. Beat the eggs, whipping cream and mustard with some salt and pepper.

4. Pour the egg mixture into the quiche pan and then add in the salmon. Sprinkle the green onions over the entire quiche. Place the quiche into the basket and then into the air fryer. Cook for 20 minutes.

Air Fryer Cookbook:

5 Ingredients or Less. Easy and Delicious Air Fryer Recipes for Your Family

Easy Crumbed Fish

Serves 4. Prep Time: 10 Mins, Cook Time: 12 Mins

Temperature: 350 °F

You will need:

4 tablespoons of vegetable oil

1 cup of breadcrumbs

1 whisked egg

4 fillets

1 lemon

Directions:

1. Begin by preheating the air fryer to 350 degrees. In a bowl you will mix the vegetable oil and the breadcrumbs, stirring until the breadcrumbs become crumbly and loose.

2. You will dip the fish in the egg and let any of the extra egg drip off. Then roll it in the crumb mixture, ensuring that the fish is completely and evenly coated.

3. Place the fish in the air fryer and cook for about 12 minutes. You may need to cook it a bit longer depending on how thick it is.

4. While the fish is cooking, slice the lemon. After the fish is cone cooking, you will place the fish on a plate as well as a lemon slice and serve.

Air Fryer Cookbook:

5 Ingredients or Less. Easy and Delicious Air Fryer Recipes for Your Family

Crab Sticks

Serves 4. Prep Time: 10 Mins, Cook Time: 10 Mins

Temperature: 320 °F

You will need

16 crab sticks

Cooking spray

Directions:

1. You will begin by unrolling each of the crab sticks and slice them into strips that are about 1 centimeter wide. Next, you will want to divide the crab onto two different plates and spray them with cooking spray. You may want to use tongs to ensure that the crab is evenly coated.

2. Next, preheat your air fryer to 320 degrees. After the air fryer has preheated for 5 minutes, you will take one plate of the crab sticks and place them in the basket then in the air fryer. Cook for 4 minutes, shake, cook for 3 minutes, shake and then cook for 3 more minutes.

3. If there are any pale colored sticks after they have cooked for 10 minutes, you will want to place them on

a separate plate. After cooking the second batch, you can cook the pale crab sticks for an additional 2 minutes.

4. Cool before serving. These can be stored for up to a week in an air-tight container.

Air Fryer Cookbook:

5 Ingredients or Less. Easy and Delicious Air Fryer Recipes for Your Family

Coconut Shrimp

Serves 2. Prep Time: 15 Mins, Cook Time: 5 - 10 Mins Temperature: 350 °F

You will need:

3 ounces of cooked shrimp that has been peeled

2 tablespoons of whole wheat flour

1/4 of a cup of unsweetened shredded coconut

1/4 of a cup of panko breadcrumbs

1 egg that has been beaten

Directions:

1. Begin by preheating your air fryer to 350 degrees.

2. Place the egg in one bowl, the flour in one bowl and in a third bowl, mix the breadcrumbs and coconut.

3. Dip each of the shrimp into the flour then dip it into the egg and then roll it in the breadcrumb mixture.

4. Place the shrimp into the air fryer basket and cook for 5 minutes (if you are working with cooked shrimp, 10 minutes if you are working with uncooked shrimp)

5. Serve the shrimp with spicy sauce.

Tilapia Fillets

Serves 2. Prep Time: 15 Mins, Cook Time: 10 Mins

Temperature: 400 °F

You will need:

3/4 of a cup of Parmesan cheese, grated

2 teaspoons of paprika

1 tablespoon of fresh parsley, chopped

Salt and pepper

4 tilapia fillets

Olive oil

Directions:

1. Begin by preheating your air fryer to 400 degrees and line your basket with a bit of foil to ensure none of the fish falls through.

2. Mix the salt, pepper, paprika and the parmesan cheese together in a dish. Use the oil to coat each of the fillets and then press the fillets into the parmesan cheese ensuring that they are coated evenly.

3. Place the fillets into the basket and place the basket into the air fryer. Cook for 10 minutes.

Air Fryer Cookbook:

5 Ingredients or Less. Easy and Delicious Air Fryer Recipes for Your Family

Fish Sticks

Serves 4. Prep Time: 10 Mins, Cook Time: 12 Mins

Temperature: 350 °F

You will need:

1 pound of Cod

2 eggs

2 cups of Panko Breadcrumbs

1/2 of a teaspoon of black pepper

1/4 of a teaspoon of sea salt

Directions:

1. Begin by mixing the eggs together in a small bowl. You will put the breadcrumbs in a second bowl with the salt and pepper.

2. Cut the Cod into sticks and dip each stick into the egg mixture. Then you will roll them in the breadcrumbs and set to the side.

3. Place the fish sticks in the fryer basket and then into the air fryer. Adjust the temperature to 350 degrees and cooking time to 12 minutes. Flip after 6 minutes and serve with tartar sauce.

Chapter 8 – Poultry recipes

BBQ chicken Drumsticks

Serves 4. Prep Time: 15 Mins, Cook Time: 30 - 60 Mins

Temperature: 300 - 400 °F

You will need:

6 drumsticks

1 bottle of your favorite BBQ sauce

Directions:

1. Begin by preheating the air fryer to 400 degrees for 5 minutes. Place the drumsticks in a bowl and coat them with the BBQ sauce.

2. After the air fryer is preheated, you will place the drumsticks in the basket and then into the air fryer. Cooking 3 at a time is going to work the best. If you have smaller drumsticks, you might be able to fit more in, but you do not want to crowd them.

3. Cook the drumsticks for 20 minutes. After they have cooked for 20 minutes, you will remove them from the air fryer and brush them with more BBQ sauce.

Air Fryer Cookbook:

5 Ingredients or Less. Easy and Delicious Air Fryer Recipes for Your Family

Reduce the heat to 300 degrees and cook for an additional 10 minutes.

4. If the drumsticks are large, you can add 3 – 5 more minutes.

5. After the drumsticks have cooked, you will want to let them sit for 5 minutes before serving.

Garlic Parmesan Chicken

Serves 4. Prep Time: 10 Mins, Cook Time: 35 Mins

Temperature: 360 °F

You will need:

2 chicken breasts cut in half

1 teaspoon of melted butter

2 garlic cloves (minced)

1 egg

1 cup of breadcrumbs

1/4 of a cup of grated Parmesan

Salt and pepper to taste

Directions:

1. Begin by preheating the air fryer to 360 degrees. Lightly spray the air fryer pan with nonstick cooking spray. While the air fryer is preheating, you will want to pound the chicken breasts to ensure that they are the same thickness.

Air Fryer Cookbook:

5 Ingredients or Less. Easy and Delicious Air Fryer Recipes for Your Family

2. Pierce the chicken breast several times with a fork. Mix the garlic, salt and pepper together and rub it on the chicken. Let this sit for about 30 minutes.

3. While this is soaking, you will place the breadcrumbs in a shallow tray and mix the breadcrumbs, parmesan, salt and pepper together.

4. Break the egg into a bowl and scramble it. After the chicken has marinated, you will dip each piece in the egg and then roll it in the breadcrumbs. After all of the pieces have been coated in breadcrumbs, you will place them in the tray. Preheat the air fryer to 360 degrees. Cook the chicken for 5 minutes and check it to see if it needs a coat of butter. Lightly brush the butter over the chicken and cook for an additional 30 minutes.

5. Serve hot with your favorite topping.

Coconut Lime Chicken

Serves 4. Prep Time: 50 Mins, Cook Time: 12 Mins Temperature: 360 °F

You will need:

4 boneless skinless chicken breasts

2 eggs

2 cups of breadcrumbs

1 cup of coarsely grated fresh coconut

Lime leaves, grated

4 tablespoons of freshly squeezed lemon juice

Salt and pepper to taste

Directions:

1. Begin by cutting the chicken breasts into long slices. Mix the lemon juice, salt, lime leaves and pepper in a bowl and marinate the chicken in the mixture for 45 minutes. While this is marinating, you will want to preheat your air fryer to 360 degrees.

2. Mix the eggs and salt in a bowl. Then mix the coconut and the breadcrumbs on a plate.

Air Fryer Cookbook:

5 Ingredients or Less. Easy and Delicious Air Fryer Recipes for Your Family

3. Place one piece of chicken in the eggs and then roll the chicken in the breadcrumbs and place it on a plate. After you have coated all of the chicken, you will arrange it in the air fryer tray that has been sprayed with nonstick cooking spray.

4. Brush each piece with a bit of oil and place in the air fryer for 9 minutes. After 9 minutes, you will want to stick a fork in the chicken and see if there is any pink still inside. If there is, any pink left, cook for 3 more minutes.

5. Serve this chicken with the dipping sauce of your choice.

Chicken Schnitzel

Serves 2. Prep Time: 15 Mins, Cook Time: 10 Mins

Temperature: 360 °F

You will need:

2 boneless skinless chicken breasts

1/2 cup of all-purpose flour

1 egg and 1 tablespoon of sesame seeds

1 tablespoon of Red chili & pepper powder

Salt

Directions:

1. Begin by cleaning the chicken breasts and then placing them in a Ziplock bag. Use a rolling pin to flatten the chicken until they are all about 1/4 of an inch thick. Set the chicken to the side.

2. Add the red chili powder, pepper powder, and the salt into the bag and shake it until all of the chicken is coated. Let this sit for 10 minutes.

3. While the chicken is marinating, you will break the egg in a small bowl and mix it with a bit of salt and pepper. Place the flour in another bowl with a bit of

Air Fryer Cookbook:

5 Ingredients or Less. Easy and Delicious Air Fryer Recipes for Your Family

salt. Place the breadcrumbs in a third bowl as well as a bit of salt. Finally, in a fourth bowl, you will place the sesame seeds.

4. To bread the chicken breasts, you will roll the chicken in the flour, dip it in the egg, roll it in the breadcrumbs and then in the sesame seeds. Batter all of the chicken and place on a plate.

5. After all of the chicken is battered, you will place it in the air fryer basket and cook it at 360 degrees for 10 minutes.

6. Serve hot.

Citrus Sage Chicken

Serves 4. Prep Time: 10 Mins, Cook Time: 13 Mins

Temperature: 360 - 390 °F

You will need:

4 boneless skinless chicken breasts

1 oranges and 1 lemons

1/4 of a cup of sage

2 tablespoons of Olive oil

1 teaspoons of salt & 1 teaspoon of black pepper

Directions:

1. Begin by grating 1 tablespoon of orange zest and squeezing 2 tablespoons of juice from the oranges. Do the exact same thing to the lemons.

2. In a large bowl, you will want to combine the orange zest, lemons zest, oil, sage, salt and the pepper. Mix well with a whisk.

3. Place the chicken in the marinade, turning it to ensure it is completely coated. Cover the chicken and marinate it for 2 hours. You will want to turn the chicken every 30 minutes.

Air Fryer Cookbook:

5 Ingredients or Less. Easy and Delicious Air Fryer Recipes for Your Family

4. After the chicken has marinated, you will preheat the air fryer to 360 degrees. Place the chicken into the air fryer basket.

5. Slice an orange in thin slices and place it on top of the chicken in and then into the air fryer. Cook the chicken for 8 minutes and then turn the chicken over. Increase the temperature to 390 degrees and cook for 5 more minutes.

6. Let the chicken rest for 5 minutes before you serve it.

Easy Whole Chicken

Serves 4 . Prep Time: 15 Mins, Cook Time: 60 Mins

Temperature: 350°F

You will need:

1 chicken that has been washed and patted dry

2 tablespoons of olive oil

1 tablespoon of seasoned salt

Directions:

1. Begin by removing the giblet pack from the inside of the chicken. Rub the oil on the outside of the entire chicken. Generously coat the outside of the chicken with the seasoned salt and rub it over the chicken. Place the chicken in the air fryer breast side down in the air fryer and cook at 350 degrees for 30 minutes.

2. After 30 minutes, remove the chicken and turn it over. Cook for an additional 30 minutes. Let the chicken rest for 10 minutes before serving.

Air Fryer Cookbook:

5 Ingredients or Less. Easy and Delicious Air Fryer Recipes for Your Family

Breaded Lemon Chicken

Serves 4 . Prep Time: 15 Mins, Cook Time: 20 Mins

Temperature: 400°F

You will need:

2 chicken breasts, boneless and skinless

1/3 of a cup of lemon juice

1.5 cups of seasoned breadcrumbs

Lemon pepper

Parsley to garnish

Directions:

1. Begin by slicing each of the chicken breasts in half, creating 4 thin chicken breasts. Place about 12 inches worth of plastic wrap on your counter and lay the chicken on top of the plastic wrap.

2. Place another layer of plastic wrap over the chicken and use a meat mallet to pound the chicken until they are about 1/4 of an inch thick.

3. Pour your vegetable oil into your frying pan, until it is about 1/4 of an inch deep.

4. Place your lemon juice in one bowl and your breadcrumbs in another. Place one chicken breast in the lemon juice bowl and allow to sit for 2 minutes. Turn the breast over and allow to sit for 2 more minutes.

5. After the breast has soaked in the lemon juice, roll it in the breadcrumbs. Continue to do the same with all of the chicken.

6. After all of the breasts have been battered, you will sprinkle them with lemon pepper and heat your air fryer to 400 degrees.

7. Place two breasts in the air fryer basket and cook for 10 minutes, shaking after 5 minutes. Then cook the second batch.

8. Serve hot, sprinkled with parsley.

Air Fryer Cookbook:

5 Ingredients or Less. Easy and Delicious Air Fryer Recipes for Your Family

Chicken Tenders

Serves 2. Prep Time: 10 Mins, Cook Time: 20 Mins Temperature: 390°F

You will need:

1 pound of chicken tenders, thawed

1/2 of a cup of panko breadcrumbs

1 egg

Directions:

1. Begin by seasoning the chicken tenders with whatever seasoning you choose to use.

2. After you have seasoned the chicken tenders, you will place the egg in one bowl and then the panko breadcrumbs in a separate bowl.

3. Dip the chicken tenders, one at a time in the egg, ensuring that both sides are coated.

4. Then roll each of the tenders in the breadcrumbs ensuring that they are evenly coated.

5. Using a bit of olive oil, spray the bottom of the air fryer pan and place 6 to 7 tenders on the tray.

6. Preheat your air fryer to 390 degrees.

7. After the air fryer has preheated, cook the tenders for 20 minutes, shaking every five minutes.

8. Serve with dipping sauce of your choice.

Air Fryer Cookbook:

5 Ingredients or Less. Easy and Delicious Air Fryer Recipes for Your Family

Chicken Bacon Meatballs

Serves 2. Prep Time: 20 Mins, Cook Time: 6 Mins

Temperature: 360°F

You will need:

500 grams of chicken that has been minced

140 grams of bacon that has been chopped finely

1 egg and 1/2 of a cup of breadcrumbs

2 tablespoons of your favorite BBQ sauce

Salt and pepper

Directions:

1. Begin by placing all of the ingredients in a large bowl and mixing them well.
2. Preheat your air fryer to 360 degrees.
3. Roll your chicken mixture into balls that are bite sized and place the balls into the air fryer basket. Place the basket in the air fryer and cook for 6 minutes, shaking after 3 minutes.
4. Serve hot.

Chicken Nuggets

Serves 4. Prep Time: 15 Mins, Cook Time: 25 Mins

Temperature: 360°F

You will need:

4 cups of all-purpose flour

6 tablespoons of garlic salt

3 tablespoons of black pepper, ground

4 beaten eggs

8 chicken breasts, boneless and skinless, cut into chunks

Directions:

1. In a bowl, mix the flour, salt, pepper, and garlic. Place the eggs in a separate bowl and beat them.

2. Dip each of the pieces of chicken into the egg and then roll it in the flour. Shake any excess flour off of the chicken.

3. Preheat your air fryer to 360 degrees and place the nuggets in the basket, cooking only one layer at a time.

Air Fryer Cookbook:

5 Ingredients or Less. Easy and Delicious Air Fryer Recipes for Your Family

4. Cook each batch for 8 minutes, shaking after 4 minutes.

5. Serve hot with your favorite dipping sauce.

Coconut Chicken Tenders

Serves 4. Prep Time: 15 Mins, Cook Time: 14 Mins

Temperature: 400°F

You will need:

8 chicken tenders

2 eggs

2 teaspoons of garlic powder

1 teaspoon of salt

1/2 of a teaspoon of black pepper, ground

3/4 of a cup of panko breadcrumbs

3/4 of a cup of sweetened shredded coconut

Directions:

1. Begin by preheating your air fryer to 400 degrees. Then place the eggs, salt, pepper and garlic powder in a shallow bowl and mix well until completely combined.

2. Place the Panko breadcrumbs and the coconut in a second dish. Mix well.

Air Fryer Cookbook:

5 Ingredients or Less. Easy and Delicious Air Fryer Recipes for Your Family

3. Dip each of the chicken tenders, one at a time into the egg, ensuring that both sides are coated evenly. Allow the excess egg to drip off and then roll the tender in the breadcrumb mixture.

4. Press the breadcrumb mixture onto the tender ensuring that it will not fall off and then place the chicken in the air fryer basket.

5. You can use a bit of coconut oil cooking spray to spray the top tenders if desired.

6. Cook for 14 minutes.

7. Serve hot with your favorite dipping sauce.

Chapter 9 - Vegetarian Recipes

One of the great things about the air fryer is that you can cook all of your favorite vegan and vegetarian recipes as well.

Air Fryer Cookbook:

5 Ingredients or Less. Easy and Delicious Air Fryer Recipes for Your Family

Cheese Veg Keto Cutlet

Serves 2 . Prep Time: 10 Mins, Cook Time: 10 Mins

Temperature: 350 °F

You will need:

2 cups of cottage cheese

1 cup of mozzarella cheese

1 onion, chopped finely

1/2 of a teaspoon of garlic powder

1/2 of a teaspoon of salt

1/2 of a teaspoon of oregano seasoning

1 teaspoon of butter

Directions:

Begin by mixing all of the ingredients in a bowl and shape them into small patties. Place the cutlets into the air fryer basket and cook at 350 degrees for 10 minutes. Serve these hot with chutney.

Veggie Balls

Serves 2 . Prep Time: 10 Mins, Cook Time: 16 Mins

Temperature: 350 °F

You will need:

200 grams of cauliflower

100 grams of sweet potatoes

70 grams of carrots

2 teaspoons of garlic puree

1 teaspoon of mixed spice

1 cup of oats

Salt and pepper

Directions:

1. Begin by placing all of the vegetables in the food processor and whirl them around until they look like breadcrumbs.

2. Place the vegetables on a kitchen towel and let the extra water drain off of them.

Air Fryer Cookbook:

5 Ingredients or Less. Easy and Delicious Air Fryer Recipes for Your Family

3. After the water has drained off, place the vegetables in a bowl and mix in the rest of the ingredients. Mix everything well and shape the mixture into balls.

4. Place the balls in the fridge and let them sit for 2 hours in the fridge so that they can firm up. After the balls have set in the fridge for 2 hours, you will preheat the air fryer to 350 degrees and cook for 8 minutes. After 8 minutes, roll the balls over and cook for another 8 minutes. Serve hot.

Crispy Tofu

Serves 4. Prep Time: 15 Mins, Cook Time: 18 Mins

Temperature: 350 °F

You will need:

8 ounces of firm tofu that has been rinsed and cut into cubes

1/2 of a teaspoon of garlic powder

1 tablespoon of brown rice flour

2 tablespoons of soy sauce

1 teaspoon of sesame oil

1 teaspoon of water

Directions:

1. Begin by combining all of the ingredients in a bowl. Mix in and stir everything together. Pour the mixture over the tofu and allow the tofu to marinate for 30 minutes covered. Sprinkle another tablespoon of brown rice flour over the tofu and mix it well.

2. Preheat the air fryer to 350 degrees and place the tofu in the basket. Cook the tofu for 18 minutes and serve hot.

Air Fryer Cookbook:

5 Ingredients or Less. Easy and Delicious Air Fryer Recipes for Your Family

Banana Chips

Serves 2. Prep Time: 10 Mins, Cook Time: 10 Mins Temperature: 350 °F

You will need:

4 raw bananas

Black pepper, salt

A bit of oil

Directions:

Begin by peeling the bananas and slicing them into thin slices. Mix the banana slices with a bit of oil, ensuring that they are all coated evenly. Place them in the air fryer basket and cook them at 350 degrees for 10 minutes. Once they have cooked, you can sprinkle them with the salt and pepper. Store these in a jar and eat within a week.

Cheese Spinach Balls

Serves 2. Prep Time: 15 Mins, Cook Time: 15 Mins Temperature: 390 °F

You will need:

300 grams of spinach leaves

Panko breadcrumbs

1 onion chopped finely

2 cups of corn flour

1.5 cup of grated mozzarella cheese

Salt

Directions:

1. Begin by boiling the spinach leaves and then placing them in your food processor to make a puree out of them. Mix the spinach puree with the corn flour, 1 cup of mozzarella and a bit of salt.

2. In order to create the filling, you will mix the onion and the rest of the mozzarella together in a bowl. Create small balls out of this. Cover the small cheese balls with the spinach puree mixture and roll them into balls.

Air Fryer Cookbook:

5 Ingredients or Less. Easy and Delicious Air Fryer Recipes for Your Family

3. After you have created the balls, you will brush all sides with a bit of oil and then cook in the air fryer for 15 minutes at 390 degrees. Serve hot with tomato sauce.

Cheeselings

Serves 4. Prep Time: 15 Mins, Cook Time: 8 Mins

Temperature: 350 °F

You will need:

1 cup of all-purpose flour

1 teaspoon of baking powder

1/4 of a teaspoon of chili powder

1 teaspoon of butter

1 cup of grated mozzarella cheese

Salt

Directions:

1. Begin by mixing the flour, a pinch of salt, baking powder, butter, chili powder, cheese and just a few drops of water in a bowl and mix well to create a stiff dough.

2. Knead the dough and then sprinkle a bit of flour on the table as well as the rolling pin. Roll out the dough into a very thin sheet and cut the dough into the shapes that you want your cheeselings to be.

Air Fryer Cookbook:

5 Ingredients or Less. Easy and Delicious Air Fryer Recipes for Your Family

3. Preheat your air fryer to 350 degrees and place the cheeselings in the basket. Cook for about 5 minutes, tossing the basket after about 2 minutes. After they have cooked for 5 minutes, toss them again and cook for an additional 3 minutes.

4. Serve with Frank's Hot Sauce.

Chapter 10- Desserts

We have covered many different types of dishes that can be made in the air fryer but did you know that you can also make all of your favorite desserts in the air fryer as well? In this chapter, I am going to give you some amazing dessert recipes that you will want to make over and over again.

Air Fryer Cookbook:

5 Ingredients or Less. Easy and Delicious Air Fryer Recipes for Your Family

Mini Pumpkin Pie Delights

Serves 4. Prep Time: 20 Mins, Cook Time: 15 Mins Temperature: 350 °F

You will need:

1 can of pumpkin pie filling

2 tablespoons of allspice

2 eggs

75 grams of all-purpose flour

33 grams of butter

15 grams of caster sugar

Directions:

1. Begin by mixing the pumpkin pie filling, allspice, and eggs in a bowl. Make sure that the everything is mixed evenly.

2. Next, you will make the pastry by mixing the flour and the butter in a bowl. Rub the butter into the flour to ensure that it mixes evenly. Next, add in the sugar and ensure that it mixes evenly. Add in a bit of water until

all of the ingredients become moist and you are able to create a dough with them.

3. Knead the dough until the texture is smooth. Next, you will butter your pastry cases. Then roll the dough out on a floured surface. Place the dough in the pastry cases just like you would the bottom of a pie pan. Fill the pastry 80 percent of the way up with the filling mix.

4. Preheat your air fryer to 350 degrees. Once the air fryer is preheated, you will place the pumpkin pies in the air fryer and cook for about 15 minutes. Let the pies rest for 5 minutes before removing them from the casing. Sit them on a cooling rack and allow to cool the rest of the way. Serve with a dollop of whipped cream.

Air Fryer Cookbook:

5 Ingredients or Less. Easy and Delicious Air Fryer Recipes for Your Family

Shortbread Fingers

Serves 2. Prep Time: 20 Mins, Cook Time: 12 Mins Temperature: 350 °F

You will need:

175 grams of butter

75 grams of caster sugar

250 grams of all-purpose flour

Directions:

1. Begin by preheating your air fryer to 350 degrees. Then place the flour and the sugar in a bowl. Mix well. Next, add in the butter and rub it into the flour/sugar mixture. Knead the mixture until it becomes a soft dough.

2. Form the dough into finger shapes, and then poke with a fork to decorate. Place them on the air fryer baking sheet that has been sprayed with nonstick spray and cook for 12 minutes.

Chocolate chip Cookie

Serves 2. Prep Time: 20 Mins, Cook Time: 20 Mins

Temperature: 350 °F

You will need:

100 grams of butter

75 grams of brown sugar

175 grams of self-rising flour

100 grams of chocolate

4 tablespoons of honey

1 tablespoon of whole milk

Directions:

1. Begin by preheating the air fryer to 350 degrees. While the air fryer is preheating, you will place the butter in a large bowl and beat it with a mixer until it is soft. Next, add in the sugar and continue to beat until they become fluffy.

2. Next, stir in the honey and the flour mixing it well.

3. Place the chocolate in a Ziploc bag and crush it with a rolling pin so that there is a mixture of large and small

Air Fryer Cookbook:

5 Ingredients or Less. Easy and Delicious Air Fryer Recipes for Your Family

chunks. Add the chocolate to the mixture a well as the milk and mix well.

4. Line the air fryer tin with parchment paper and then spoon the cookie dough into the tin. Cook this for 20 minutes and then let cool before cutting and serving.

Flourless Chocolate Cake

Serves 1 cake. Prep Time: 1 hour and 35 Mins, Cook Time: 35 Mins

Temperature: 350 °F

You will need:

10 ripe bananas

10 teaspoons of cocoa powder

4 tablespoons of honey

1 avocado

8 eggs

Directions:

1. Begin by preheating your air fryer to 350 degrees. Then place all of the ingredients except for the avocado in a blender. Blend all of the ingredients until they are smooth.

2. Place enough of the mixture to use for the icing to the side and then place the rest in two cake pans.

3. Place the cake pans in the air fryer and cook for 35 minutes.

Air Fryer Cookbook:

5 Ingredients or Less. Easy and Delicious Air Fryer Recipes for Your Family

4. While the cakes are cooking you will mix the rest of the batter with the avocado until it becomes a thick paste.

5. After the cakes have cooked you will place a thin layer of the icing on one of the cakes and then place the other cake on top.

6. Use the rest of the icing to frost the cake and place in the fridge for at least one hour allowing the icing to set.

Chocolate Mug Cake

Serves 2 . Prep Time: 5 Mins, Cook Time: 10 Mins

Temperature: 400 °F

You will need:

1/4 of a cup of self-rising flour

5 tablespoons of caster sugar

1 tablespoon of cocoa powder

3 teaspoons of coconut oil, melted

3 tablespoons of whole milk

Directions:

1. Begin by placing all of the ingredients in a mug (oven safe) and mixing them well. Preheat the air fryer to 400 degrees.

2. After the air fryer has heated up, place the mug in and allow to cook for 10 minutes. Serve hot.

Air Fryer Cookbook:

5 Ingredients or Less. Easy and Delicious Air Fryer Recipes for Your Family

Butter Cookies

Serves 2. Prep Time: 30 Mins, Cook Time: 14 Mins

Temperature: 300 °F

You will need:

70 grams of all-purpose flour

50 grams of butter, unsalted

20 grams of caster sugar

Directions:

1. Begin by creaming the butter and the sugar together. Next, add in the flour and mix well until the dough forms. It should be soft.

2. Wrap the dough in plastic wrap and then place it in the freezer for between 15 to 30 minutes allowing it to become firm.

3. After the dough has become firm, Weigh out 10 grams of the dough and shape it into the shape that you want your cookies to be.

4. Place the cookies into the air fryer, set the temperature to 300 degrees and cook for 14 minutes. They should come out golden brown.

5. Allow to cool and serve.

Easy Banana Chips

Serves 2. Prep Time: 30 Mins, Cook Time: 14 Mins

Temperature: 400 °F

You will need:

3 green bananas

1 cup of water

1 teaspoon of turmeric

Salt

Non-stick Coconut oil spray if desired, used for flavor

Directions:

1. Begin washing the bananas, do not peel them but instead, wash the peels and then set them to the side.

2. Next, mix the water, turmeric and the salt in a bowl.

3. Cut the bananas into slices that are about 1/2 of a centimeter thick. If you cut the slices too thin, they will burn in the air fryer and if they are too thick, they are not going to be crisp.

4. Place the banana slices in the turmeric water mixture and allow them to soak for about 15 minutes.

Air Fryer Cookbook:

5 Ingredients or Less. Easy and Delicious Air Fryer Recipes for Your Family

5. Drain the excess liquid off of the bananas and set them to the side. Allow them to begin drying. Preheat the air fryer to 400 degrees.

6. Place one layer of banana slices in the air fryer basket and place the basket in the air fryer. Cook for 14 minutes, shaking the basket after five minutes.

7. Allow the chips to cool and serves.

Conclusion

I hope that you have enjoyed this book as well as all of the recipes in it. I also hope that you have learned through reading all of the recipes in this book that you can still enjoy all of your favorite foods while still eating healthy and reducing not only the fat but the calories that are in all of the foods that you love.

The air fryer is not only going to help you create delicious foods without using fat, but it is also going to help you to become a healthier and happier person. Now you can prepare healthy meals for your family in almost no time at all, without having to worry about the fat that you would normally find in these foods.

One of the greatest things about the air fryer is that you can cook almost anything in it and never lose any of the flavors.

Now head on into that kitchen, pull that air fryer out and start making some of these delicious recipes!

Air Fryer Cookbook:

5 Ingredients or Less. Easy and Delicious Air Fryer Recipes for Your Family

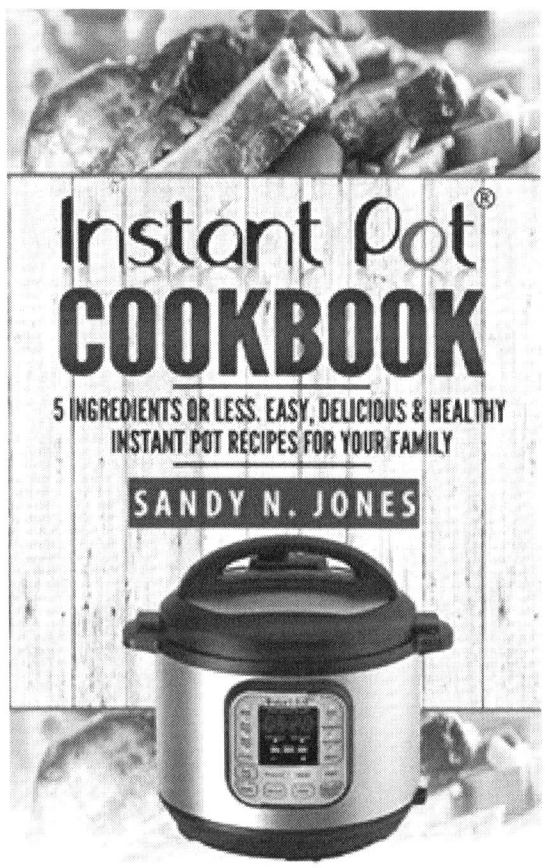

5 Ingredients or Less. Easy, Delicious & Healthy Instant Pot Recipes for Your Family

This book is packed full of recipes for breakfast, lunch, and dinner that only take five ingredients or less to prepare. On top of that, the majority of the recipes in this book will only take you 20 minutes or less to make.

Did you enjoy reading this book? Can I ask you a favour?

Thanks for purchasing and reading this book, I really hope you find it helpful.

If you find this book helpful, **<u>please help others find this book by kindly leaving a review.</u>** I love getting feedback from my customers, I would really appreciate your thoughts.

Printed in Great Britain
by Amazon